Dear Jennifer and Ben ♥

Thank you for your [...]
and thoughtfulness!

Love,
Aunt Julie

THIS ABRIDGED EDITION
MADE EXCLUSIVELY FOR

BY THE
BALLANTINE PUBLISHING
GROUP

ONENESS

GREAT PRINCIPLES
SHARED BY ALL

JEFFREY MOSES

BALLANTINE BOOKS • NEW YORK

http://www.randomhouse.com

Library of Congress Cataloging
in Publication Data: 97-92970

ISBN: 0-345-41253-2

Cover design by Barbara Leff

Manufactured in the United States of America
First Ballantine Books/Hallmark Edition:
May 1997

10 9 8 7 6 5 4 3 2 1

To Ruth, whose love and devotion
helped bring this book to light.

Every major religion of the world has similar ideals of love, the same goal of benefitting humanity through spiritual practice, and the same effect of making their followers into better human beings. As this book shows, the great religious teachers wanted to lead people away from the paths of misdeeds caused by ignorance and introduce them to paths of goodness.

THE DALAI LAMA

CONTENTS

FOREWORD

Throughout the ages, the scriptures of all religions have proclaimed that humanity is one great family. This is a simple truth, and it is simply and directly stated in every religion. In fact, almost all the principles that are associated with religious thought are shared by every religion. The Golden Rule, Love Thy Neighbor, Honor Thy Father and Mother, It Is More Blessed to Give Than to Receive—these principles and others are common to all religions and are very similarly expressed in each.

This book discusses many of these fundamental precepts and shows their similarity of expression. Each page was put together with the awareness that modern words can hardly add to the immensity of the world's collected spiritual wisdom. For this reason the commentaries are short, allowing the sayings to speak for themselves.

The principles in this book form the basis

for structuring an individual's life. The great sayings are like a guide or a blueprint for the inner development of mind and spirit that allows a person to achieve his highest goals. These principles are the foundation for success in personal relationships with family and friends, for satisfaction and success in business activities, and for that final aspiration in life that each person ultimately desires—the achievement of inner peace extending beyond the confines of an individual lifetime.

These great principles are not limiting to a person's satisfaction and fulfillment. Instead, they are guidelines that enable men and women to evolve to the highest point of human consciousness, wherein oneness is achieved with all the laws of nature. They allow men to avoid mistakes, to take the path of growth and achievement, and to answer the urgent and vital questions that ultimately arise.

Many people today seek their own laws. Yet in so doing, they often find only partial values of these universal principles. In actuality, the full values of these universal principles have been recorded similarly in all major religions since time immemorial. The principles of inner development are basically no different now than they were in the days of Jesus, Buddha, Muhammad, Shankara, or Confucious. These great masters offer similar messages that have not become less essential for people in the modern world. These principles stretch beyond time and change. They establish a clearly marked path which will enable each individual to attain the peace and enlightenment that is the ultimate goal in life.

THE GOLDEN RULE

The Golden Rule is the cornerstone of religious understanding. Such diverse principles as *Love Thy Neighbor, Honor Thy Father and Mother, Speak Truth, Judge Not, Do Not Harm Anyone,* and *It Is More Blessed to Give Than To Receive*—among many others—are reflections of The Golden Rule. Abiding by The Golden Rule in thought and in deed naturally evokes the expression of all these other principles.

The Golden Rule is the most succinct and all-embracing description of how individuals and nations should act toward their neighbors. Every religion considers The Golden Rule to be the highest expression of spiritual thought. The founders of every major world religion—among them Jesus, Buddha, Krishna, Confucius, and Muhammad—all taught that following The Golden Rule is the surest way for mankind to fulfill its most cherished ideals.

THE GOLDEN RULE

Do unto others as you would have them do unto you, for this is the law and the prophets.

Christianity

What is hurtful to yourself do not to your fellow man. That is the whole of the Torah and the remainder is but commentary.

Judaism

Do unto all men as you would wish to have done unto you; and reject for others what you would reject for yourselves.

Islam

Hurt not others with that which pains
yourself.

Buddhism

Tzu-Kung asked: "Is there one principle
upon which one's whole life may proceed?"
The Master replied, "Is not Reciprocity
such a principle?—what you do not
yourself desire, do not put before others."

Confucianism

This is the sum of all true righteousness—
Treat others, as thou wouldst thyself be
    treated.
Do nothing to thy neighbor, which
    hereafter
Thou wouldst not have thy neighbor do to
    thee.

Hinduism

7

HONOR THY FATHER
AND MOTHER

It would be difficult to repay our parents for the hours, days, and years they cared for us when we were young. Perhaps the only way to return some of that love is through caring for our own children, and for our parents as they grow older.

We should do our best to know our parents, for knowing them is the key to knowing ourselves. The day will come when we shall wish we had known them better.

HONOR THY FATHER
AND MOTHER

My son, keep your father's commandment,
and forsake not your mother's teaching.
Bind them upon your heart always; tie
them about your neck. When you walk,
they will lead you; when you lie down, they
will watch over you; and when you awake,
they will talk with you.

Judaism

For God commanded, saying, Honor thy
father and mother.

Christianity

Honor thy Father and Mother. Forget not
the favours thou hast received.

Hinduism

Serve and revere your parents. Heaven is
spread beneath the feet of mothers
everywhere.

Islam

To support Father and Mother,
To cherish Wife and Child,
To follow a peaceful calling,
This is the greatest blessing.

Buddhism

If each man would love his parents and
show due respect to his elders, the whole
empire would enjoy tranquillity.

Confucianism

—

MORE BLESSED TO
GIVE THAN TO RECEIVE

The wise handling of money can be as spiritually enriching as prayer. A person who is in touch with his own inner self and who truly loves his fellow man will experience his heart spontaneously overflowing with the desire to care for others.

The giving of money, time, support, and encouragement to worthy causes can never be detrimental to the giver. The laws of nature are structured so that acts of charity will open an individual to an unbounded reservoir of riches. Everything in life has been created as the result of love and concern for others. When individuals give lovingly to their brothers in the family of man, they establish the basis for peace within every nation.

MORE BLESSED TO
GIVE THAN TO RECEIVE

It is more blessed to give than to receive.

Christianity

Extend your help without seeking reward.
Give to others and do not regret or
begrudge your liberality. Those who are
thus are good.

Taoism

In the minds of the generous contentment
is produced.

Sikhism

The poor, the orphan, the captive—feed them for the love of God alone, desiring no reward, nor even thanks.

Islam

Bounteous is he who gives to the beggar who comes to him in want of food and feeble.

Hinduism

Blessed is he that considereth the poor: the Lord will deliver him in time of trouble.

Judaism

LOVE THY NEIGHBOR

Every human being is born with an innate love for others. As a person matures, this love is put to many tests. Yet by understanding the teachings of the world's great religions, a person can find the faith he needs for his love to endure beyond life's hardships.

More than a passing glance at the scriptures is necessary to achieve this level of understanding. Acts of faith, prayer, and deep meditation provide us with the strength that allows love for our fellow man to become an abiding part of our lives, of our beings. When many of us attain this type of faith, the expression of love in the world will be as spontaneous and natural as love between mother and child.

LOVE THY NEIGHBOR

Thou shalt love thy neighbor as thyself.

Judaism

A new commandment I give to you, That you love one another; even as I have loved you . . . By this all men will know that you are my disciples, if you have love for one another.

Christianity

A man obtains a proper rule of action by looking on his neighbor as himself.

Hinduism

Full of love for all things in the world,
practicing virtue in order to benefit others,
this man alone is happy.

Buddhism

Seek to be in harmony with all your
neighbors; live in amity with your brethren.

Confucianism

Regard Heaven as your father, Earth as
your mother, and all things as your
brothers and sisters.

Shintoism

CONQUER
WITH LOVE

Whenever there is tension or fighting between individuals, groups, or nations, it means that a time of mutual understanding has been lost, and channels of communication have not been used.

Love is a unifying force. It radiates outward to resolve differences between people and nations. It is not that these unique qualities dissolve and are lost, but that they are integrated into a greater whole in which they are made more useful and beautiful.

Love conquers *before* there is fighting. Even if channels of communication have broken down and fighting breaks out, the underlying attitude should still be one of love and unification by love.

CONQUER
WITH LOVE

Recompense evil, conquer it, with good.

Islam

Be not overcome of evil, but overcome evil
with good.

Christianity

With kindness conquer rage, with goodness
malice; with generosity defeat all meanness;
with the straight truth defeat lies and
deceit.

Hinduism

A soft answer turns away wrath, but a
harsh word stirs up anger.

Judaism

Conquer your foe by force, and you
increase his anger. Conquer by love, and
you will reap no after-sorrow.

Buddhism

Love is sure to be victorious even in battle,
and firmly to maintain its ground. Heaven
will save its possessor, by his love
protecting him.

Taoism

23

BLESSED ARE THE PEACEMAKERS

When people live in the awareness that there is a close kinship between all individuals and nations, peace is the natural result. Peace can come about only as a result of concern and understanding for others. It can never be brought about by superficial negotiation or temporary agreement.

Peace certainly cannot be brought about by signatures on pieces of paper. Since the beginning of recorded history, tens of thousands of peace treaties have been signed between nations. Clearly, treaties cannot sustain peace. This is a lesson that must be learned finally and absolutely. It is time now to look toward deeper, more lasting feelings of love and understanding between people. This and this alone can bring sustained harmony in the world.

BLESSED ARE THE PEACEMAKERS

Blessed are the peacemakers: for they shall
be called the children of God.

Christianity

Shall I tell you what acts are better than
fasting, charity, and prayers? Making peace
between enemies are such acts; for enmity
and malice tear up the heavenly rewards by
the roots.

Islam

The noble minded dedicate themselves to
the promotion of peace and the happiness
of others—even those who injure them.

Hinduism

When righteousness is practiced to win
peace, he who so walks shall gain the
victory and all fetters utterly destroy.

Buddhism

How beautiful upon the mountains are the
feet of him who brings good tidings, who
publishes peace.

Judaism

AS YE SOW, SO
SHALL YE REAP

This is the great mystery of human life. This principle is so fundamental to each person's desires and goals that it forms a framework for activity throughout the day. For those who are aware that this principle is the determining factor in achieving happiness and success, the hours of the day become an attempt to act toward others with kindness and rightness. Those who are unaware struggle continuously throughout their lives and do not know why. Aware or unaware, all are ruled by this inevitable law of nature.

AS YE SOW, SO
SHALL YE REAP

It is nature's rule, that as we sow, we shall
reap.

Buddhism

Whatever a man sows, that he will also
reap.

Christianity

A liberal man will be enriched, and one
who waters will himself be watered.

Judaism

What proceeds from you will return to you.

Confucianism

Thou canst not gather what thou dost not sow; as thou dost plant the tree so it will grow.

Hinduism

Whatever man soweth, that shall he reap. If he soweth trouble, trouble shall be his harvest. If a man sow poison, he cannot expect ambrosia.

Sikhism

A MAN IS KNOWN BY HIS DEEDS, NOT BY HIS RELIGION

Inner life is the basis for outer activity. A person's actions are the mirror of his inner self. For this reason, when a man achieves an understanding of the spiritual aspects of human life, he spontaneously acts in a manner that encourages and supports a similar development of this knowledge in others. We need look no deeper than a man's outer activity to see the degree of his inner spiritual achievement.

A MAN IS KNOWN BY HIS DEEDS, NOT BY HIS RELIGION

God will not ask a man of what race he is. He will ask what he has done.

Sikhism

God will render to every man according to his deeds.

Christianity

A man asked Muhammad how to tell when one is truly faithful, and he replied: "If you derive pleasure from the good which you do and are grieved by the evil which you commit, then you are a true believer."

Islam

But I say unto you: deeds of love are worth
as much as all the commandments of the
law.

Judaism

No brahmin is a brahmin by birth.
No outcaste is an outcaste by birth.
An outcaste is an outcaste by his deeds.
A brahmin is a brahmin by his deeds.

Buddhism

NOT WORDS OR DETACHMENT, BUT ACTION

It is necessary, and perhaps one of our primary tasks on earth, to actively resolve the differences and disagreements between people.

Each person should have the goal to depart from this life having removed from the world all need for locks and keys and weapons and armor.

This goal may be too idealistic for many people—yet if no one on earth holds such an ideal, a state of peace and harmony will never reign on earth.

NOT WORDS OR DETACHMENT, BUT ACTION

Not everyone that sayeth, Lord, Lord, shall enter into the kingdom of heaven; but he that doeth the will of my Father which is in heaven.

Christianity

Not learning but doing is the chief thing.

Judaism

Not in words does God get answers.

Taoism

Students and teachers, and all others,
Who read the mere words of ponderous
　　books, know nothing,
But only waste their time in vain pursuit of
　　words;
He who acts righteously is wise.

Hinduism

Like a beautiful flower, full of color, but
without scent, are the fine but fruitless
words of him who does not act
accordingly.

Buddhism

BETTER TO
EXAMINE THE SELF

Our activities and successes are based on our inner strength and wholeness. To grow, it is necessary for us to recognize and correct our own faults. Yet it is difficult to do this since we hide our shortcomings not only from others but from ourselves.

When we gain the ability to recognize and correct our own bad habits, we begin to make rapid strides toward greater happiness and success in all spheres of life. Only by learning to admit to our own faults can we become more tolerant and loving to our fellow man and to his shortcomings.

BETTER TO
EXAMINE THE SELF

If you love others, and affection is not
returned, look into your love. If you rule
others, and they are unruly, look into your
wisdom. If you treat others politely, and
they do not return your politeness, look
into your respect. If your desires are not
fulfilled, turn inward and examine yourself.

Confucianism

First take the log out of your own eye, and
then you will see clearly to take the speck
out of your brother's eye.

Christianity

The faults of others we see easily; our own are very difficult to see. Our neighbour's faults we winnow eagerly, as chaff from grain; our own we hide away as a cheat hides a losing roll of the dice.

Buddhism

He who knows others is discerning; he who knows himself is wise.

Taoism

They who quarrel with others, instead of quarreling with their own hearts, waste their lives.

Sikhism

MAN DOES NOT LIVE BY BREAD ALONE

The blessings of life are deeper than what can be appreciated by the senses. All activities, all successes, all well-being and happiness, have their basis in an unfathomable Spirit which sustains us even when we are not aware of it.

The fullest expression of this Spirit is found in loving relationships between people. Life is nourished by kindness, by concern for others, by forgiving, by sharing, and by caring for all of God's creatures. Man does not live by material bread alone. He lives by a deeper power. The closer a person can come toward harmony with this power—with this spirit of the Divine—the more joy life will have for him.

MAN DOES NOT LIVE BY BREAD ALONE

Man shall not live by bread alone, but by
every word of God.

Christianity

Man lives not by material bread alone.

Hinduism

Make divine knowledge thy food.

Sikhism

Man doth not live by bread only, but by every word that proceedeth out of the mouth of the Lord.

Judaism

The superior man deliberates upon how he may walk in truth, not upon what he may eat.

Confucianism

DO NOT HARM
ANYTHING

Just as we try to nourish and strengthen ourselves, so we should do the same for others. If someone tries to hurt another, it means that he is perceiving that person as something separate and foreign from himself.

We must remember that the feelings and hopes of others are the same as ours. Do not forget that all religions—which convey mankind's highest thoughts and aspirations—view all the people in the world as one great family.

DO NOT HARM
ANYTHING

Do not hurt others, do no one injury by
thought or deed, utter no word to pain thy
fellow creatures.

Hinduism

Hurt none by word or deed, be consistent
in well-doing.

Buddhism

Be ye kind to one another, tenderhearted,
forgiving one another, even as God for
Christ's sake hath forgiven you.

Christianity

Master of his senses and avoiding wrong,
one should do no harm to any living being,
neither by thoughts nor words nor acts.

Jainism

Whatever good you do for others, you send
it before your own soul and shall find it
with God, who sees all you do.

Islam

BE SLOW
TO ANGER

Anger clouds the mind in the very moments that clarity and objectivity are needed most. Anger is the enemy of success and satisfaction. It rips apart the contented feeling in the mind. The more a person can stand apart and control sudden anger, the greater the chance for success in any undertaking, and the greater the chance for lasting fulfillment in life.

In the deepest sense, anger shows that a person feels he or she alone—not God—is responsible for the end result of an activity. Such a person can become very frustrated when obstacles suddenly arise. By remembering that there are many elements involved in success over which a person has little control, he can learn to diminish the fire of anger.

It has been said that when angry with loved ones, a person should count to ten before speaking. Actually, counting to ten is

not long enough. Don't speak until calm-
ness has been regained. If this takes an
hour, or several hours, it is better than saying something that may be deeply regretted.

BE SLOW
TO ANGER

He who is slow to anger has great
understanding, but he who has a hasty
temper exalts folly.

Judaism

He who gives up anger attains to God.

Hinduism

Let not the sun go down upon your wrath.

Christianity

Let us cease from wrath and refrain from angry gestures.

Shintoism

He who holds back rising anger like a rolling chariot, him I call a real driver; others only hold the reins.

Buddhism

START WHEN YOUNG
TO SEEK WISDOM

When a seed germinates, it first sends a root downward into the earth. Only when the root is firmly established do limbs and branches begin to form. When constructing a skyscraper that will tower hundreds of feet in the air, builders first dig into the ground. Only when the foundation is complete does upward construction begin.

The same is true in a young person's growth. The stronger and more orderly the inner preparation, the greater the chance for fulfillment in life.

A great step is taken toward success and happiness when one becomes able to learn from the advice of others, not only from one's own successes and failures. Until that time, progress will be slow, and unnecessary suffering will result.

The most important advice to be understood and followed is the collected wisdom

of the world's religions. This wisdom allows
a person to establish an inner foundation for
success and happiness. The younger a person
is when he becomes aware of this, the easier
it will be to accomplish all he wants in life.

START WHEN YOUNG
TO SEEK WISDOM

My son, gather instruction from thy youth
up; so shalt thou find wisdom till thine old
age.

Judaism

Knowledge is riches, what one learns in
youth is engraven on stone.

Hinduism

Seek ye first the kingdom of God, and His
righteousness; and all these things shall be
added unto you.

Christianity

Seek knowledge from the cradle to the grave.

Islam

He who, even as a young student, applies himself to the doctrine of truth, brightens up this world like the moon set free from the clouds.

Buddhism

BE WHOLEHEARTED

All success in life is the result of putting our attention into the proper channels and allowing a natural growth to occur. It is far too easy to let the mind remain divided, thinking about one thing or another, while trying to accomplish something important.

Working with a divided mind almost always gives results that are less than hoped for. But when a direct course is taken and a task is undertaken with dynamic, one-pointed perseverance, we can overcome even the most difficult obstacles.

BE WHOLEHEARTED

Wheresoever you go, employ all your heart.

Confucianism

He who doubts is like a wave of the sea that is driven and tossed by the wind.

Christianity

Whatever your hand finds to do, do it with your might.

Judaism

Free yourself from doubt and you will find
your life quickened in the goodness of
God.

Shintoism

Neither eating, nor fasting, nor penance,
nor sacrifice, nor observance of the
seasons, purify a mortal who has not
conquered his doubt.

Buddhism

HONOR THE ELDERLY

It is not in nature's plan for the elderly to be overly active in society, but they contribute in very important ways to the achievements of a nation. The gathered knowledge of the elderly in practical matters is immense. No person who has specific goals and aspirations should disregard the advice of these experienced individuals.

The more the aspirations of a society are based on the true nature of happiness—the lasting inner oneness with all things—the more a society will honor its aged members. Wisdom fills the elderly like water fills a reservoir. For this wellspring to flow, we must maintain a pipeline of respect.

HONOR THE ELDERLY

He who always greets and constantly reveres the aged, four things will increase to him: life, beauty, happiness, power.

Buddhism

With the ancient is wisdom; and in length of days understanding.

Judaism

Treat with reverence due to age the elders in your own family.

Confucianism

Rebuke not an elder, but intreat him as a father.

Christianity

To honor an old man is to show respect for God.

Islam

LIVING IN
UNITY

Fostering growth and development is as natural to a society as desiring advancement in life is to an individual. The greater the harmony and peace in a nation, the greater is the opportunity for firmly established financial, spiritual, and educational organizations to develop. These organizations allow individuals and the society as a whole to progress.

The joy of living in society is that each person can derive benefits from every other person's efforts. Each person contributes a little, and then receives the vast benefit of society's achievements.

Material needs and comforts are only one aspect of this collective benefit; a greater aspect is the collective wisdom of the spiritual truths that are passed from generation to generation. This wisdom serves as a practical basis for achieving fulfillment in life.

LIVING IN UNITY

God hath made of one blood all nations of men.

Christianity

Behold, how good and pleasant it is when brothers dwell in unity!

Judaism

All creatures are the family of God; and he is the most beloved of God who does most good unto His family.

Islam

Human beings all are as head, arms, trunk, and legs unto one another.

Hinduism

Do not forget that the world is one great family.

Shintoism

About the Author

JEFFREY MOSES has an M.A. in the philosophy of education from the University of Colorado. A freelance writer and advertising executive, Moses has spent the last ten years researching the world's great scriptures. He has traveled across the country lecturing to college and business people on the benefits of meditation and stress reduction techniques.

Jeffrey Moses and his wife, Ruth live in the Midwestern United States.